Children's Prayers for All Occasions

Rev. LAWRENCE G. LOVASIK, S.V.D.
Divine Word Missionary

Nihil Obstat: James T. O'Connor, S.T.D., Censor Librorum
Imprimatur: ✠ Patrick J. Sheridan, D.D., Vicar General, Archdiocese of New York

Prayer on Awaking

O MY God,
I offer You
through the Immaculate Heart of Mary
all my thoughts, words, actions, and
sufferings
of this day.

I offer them
to please You, to honor You,
and to make up for my sins.

Sweet Mother Mary,
keep me in your care.

Prayers during the Day

D EAR Jesus,
help me to say little prayers to You
during the day:

- Thanks be to God.

- My Lord and my God.

- Praised be Jesus Christ.

- Lord Jesus, bless all the children of the world.

Prayer before Meals

B LESS us, O Lord,
and these, Your gifts,
which we are about to receive from Your
goodness,
through Christ our Lord.
Amen.

Prayer before Going to Bed

MY God and Father,
I thank You for all the blessings
You have given me today.

I am sorry for all my sins,
because they have hurt You.

Bless my father and mother,
my brothers and sisters,
my relatives and friends,
and all who need Your help.

Prayer before Going to Confession

JESUS, my Lord and my God,
   I am sorry for all my sins
   because they have offended You.

You died on the Cross
   because of my sins.

I want to try hard
   to keep away from sin,
   so that I may always be Your friend
   and show You that I really love You.

Prayer before Mass and Communion

JESUS, my Lord,
   You give Yourself to me
   as Food in Holy Communion.
   You offer Yourself for me
   in every Holy Mass
   as You did upon the Cross.

I adore You as my God
      in the Sacrament of the Altar
      where Your Heart is all on fire
      with deepest love for me.

8

Prayer for Easter Sunday

JESUS, You are the Son of God,
and You rose from the dead on Easter
Sunday.

You saved us from sin and the devil,
brought us joy and peace,
and gave us new life and hope.

All the things God the Father made on earth
are beautiful:
the sun and sky, fields and meadows,
flowers and trees, birds and animals.

He made them all for His glory
and to make us happy.
But He did not make us for this world;
He made us for heaven.

I am a child of God.
You gave me Your own life of grace
in Baptism.
My soul is more beautiful in Your eyes
than the whole world.

Help me to praise the Father
by being His loving child
and by loving You as my Brother.

Prayer for Christmas Day

JESUS, my God,
    for love of me,
    You were born of the Virgin Mary
    and became a child like me.

You wanted to work and suffer,
    and even to die on the Cross,
    to show Your love for me
    and to save my soul.

When I look into the crib,
    I ask You, Mary, and Joseph
    to bless my family.

When I see the beautiful Christmas tree
    with lights and ornaments,
    I think of how beautiful my soul should be
    in the grace of God
    and that I will live forever.

When I see the toys I received,
    I think of the many wonderful things
    You have done for me.

Prayer on Mary's Feasts

BLESSED Virgin Mary,
Jesus gave you to me
as my Mother
when He was dying on the Cross.

I want to love you as Jesus did.

I pray to you in these words:

Hail Mary, full of grace!
The Lord is with you;
blessed are you among women,
and blessed is the fruit
of your womb, Jesus.

Holy Mary, Mother of God,
pray for us sinners,
now and at the hour
of our death. Amen.

Prayer before Studying

Dear Jesus,
    I want to study hard for You,
    because this is what You want.

Send me Your Holy Spirit
    to give me light and help
    in all my studies,
    especially in my Catechism.

I want You to be
    my best Friend.
    Take me to heaven some day.

Prayer before Going out to Play

Dear Jesus,
 You were once a child like me
 and had friends to play with You.

Bless me and all the friends You gave me.
 Help us to be kind to each other
 when we play.

Keep us from all that is bad
 that we may all be Your friends
 and be pleasing to our Heavenly Father.

Prayer for My Family

Dear Jesus,
I thank You
for the good mother and father
You gave me.

I thank You
for my brothers and sisters,
for my home,
for my food and clothes,
and for all the good things I receive.

Bless my parents
for all they do for me.
Give them grace and health
now on earth.

Then in heaven
give them a great reward—
give them Your own dear Self.

Give our family peace and love,
so that we may have a happy home.
Help us to do Your will
and meet in heaven again.

Prayer in Time of Sadness

Dear Jesus,
   I am sad but I offer my pain to You
   because You suffered on the Cross for me.

When I do something wrong,
   help me always to admit it
   and take my punishment.

You are my best Friend when I need help.
   I know You will never leave me.

Prayer in Time of Joy

My Lord Jesus,
I am especially happy today
and I thank You that I feel so good.

I also thank You
for all the great things
You have done for me.

Keep me close to You
until I am with You in heaven
where my joy will never end.

Prayer on Holidays

L ord God,
I give You thanks
for letting me live
in this great land,
which is filled with good things.

Thank You
for letting me be free
to live in peace
and to worship You without fear.

Take care of our President
and let him be a good ruler.

Watch over our other leaders in government
and help them to make just laws.

Help all the citizens of our country
to follow Your holy Will
and to live in love for each other
and for You.

Let us enjoy this holiday
by being refreshed in mind and body
so that we may continue to serve You
every day of our lives.

Prayer on Sundays

D ear Lord,
Sunday is a special day.
It is set aside for us to thank and praise You,
especially at Holy Mass.

Help me to rest from the usual things I do
and think about God and the things of God.

Make everyone in my family be happy,
and let us be good to other people.

Prayer on Weekdays

Dear Lord,
this day is a gift from You;
let me make good use of it.

Help me to do what I have to do
so that I may grow in body, mind, and soul.

Every day, let me know You more,
love You deeper,
and serve You better
so that I may be happy with You
forever in heaven.

Prayer on Receiving Toys

D ear Jesus,
I thank You for the toys
that my parents buy for me.

When You were a Child,
I am sure that You also had toys
that Your Mother Mary and St. Joseph gave
You.

When I play with my toys,
I feel very happy
and close to You,
dear Jesus.

I know
that many children in the world are poor
and have no toys to play with.
Please help these children.

Help me to thank my parents
for the nice things they buy for me
by praying for them.

All they want is that I love them
and try hard to be very good.

Prayer of Thanks for Jesus' Gifts

Dear Jesus,
I thank You for the many things
You give me each day
to make me happy.

The radio brings me the music I like.
Television lets me see beautiful things
that You have made in the world.

Let me learn from the good things
that I see and hear,
but keep me from watching
whatever may harm my soul.

Teach me how to enjoy Your many gifts
and use them to help me
love You more
and serve You better.

May my greatest joy be in You,
my best Friend.

When I study or work or play,
let it be all for You.

Prayer when Playing with My Pets

J esus, I thank You for the many things
  You give me that make my life happy.

You give me the little animals
  to be my companions.

They remind me
  of how much You care for me.

I want to be kind to my pets
  and to all animals
  because You made them to give You glory.

Prayer on My Name Day

Dear Saint N.,
I have been honored to bear your name,
which you made famous by your holiness.
Help me never to shame this name.

Obtain God's grace for me
that I may grow in faith, hope, and love,
and all the virtues.

Grant that by imitating you I may imitate
your Lord and Master, Jesus Christ.

Watch over me all my life
and bring me safe to my heavenly home.

Prayer on My Birthday

Dear Jesus, I thank You
    for each day of my life;
    it is a gift from You.

Help me to use it well
    to serve You
    and the people I meet each day.

Thank You especially for this day,
    which is my birthday,
    my special day.

It reminds me
    of the great love You have for me—
    a love that gave me life
    and many other good things.

Grant me always Your love
    that I may grow
    in wisdom, knowledge, and grace
    with every passing day.

When my life on earth is over,
    take me to heaven
    to live with You forever.

Prayer before the Blessed Sacrament

J esus, I thank You
for staying in the tabernacle
to be with me and to hear my prayers.

You are my best Friend;
I want to visit You often
and tell You that I love You.

O Sacrament most holy,
O sacrament divine!
All praise and all thanksgiving
be every moment Thine!